The Peacemakers

The Peacemakers David A. Andelman

Issues and Perspectives: A New York Times Resource Library

Harper & Row, Publishers
1817
New York   Evanston   San Francisco   London

Issues and Perspectives: A New York Times
Resource Library is a joint venture with
Harper & Row, Publishers to bring a series of
books on contemporary issues to the schools
of the United States.

Contents

Only a peace between equals can last. Only a peace the very principle of which is equality and a common participation in a common benefit.

Woodrow Wilson, 1917

Chapter One The Quest for a Permanent Peace

The year was 1919. The world, or at least most of the world, had just finished five years of war. And now its leaders were gathering in Paris to make the peace—or divide the spoils of war, depending upon one's vantage point.

It was the first of many peacemaking attempts to be held in the twentieth century in this city of towering cathedrals and sparkling rivers. In many respects 1919 was a turning point, and the peacemakers who gathered in Paris were the harbingers of a new era, whether they knew it or not.

At least one man did know it. He was Woodrow Wilson, president of the United States, who two years earlier when his country entered World War I had declared that it would be the "war to end all wars." It was an idealistic crusade, but in 1919 Wilson's was a unique departure from the nineteenth century concept of war.

Prior to World War I the major powers of Europe generally fought polite, though often bloody "little wars," chiefly for the purpose of territorial aggrandizement or to replace a ruler unpopular with a certain faction.

The governing motives of most diplomats were similar to those of Count Otto von Bismarck of Prussia whose concept of *realpolitik* included the notion that one should grab as much as possible of the spoils of war. But Woodrow Wilson wanted something more to emerge from the battlefields of the First World War. It was the bloodiest war that had been waged to date and had involved more countries and more casualties than any previous conflict. Wilson wanted a peace that would prevent any such holocausts.

Wilson's fellow peacemakers at Paris saw their missions differently. British Prime Minister David Lloyd George, French Premier Georges Clemenceau, and Italian Premier Vittorio Emanuele Orlando were diplomats of the Bismarckian school, raised in the baroque intrigues of nineteenth century European diplomacy and schooled in the art of dividing the spoils.

The Paris Peace Conference of 1919 was the last of the old-style peace conferences in that *realpolitik* played a crucial role in influencing the outcome. But it was also the first of a new style of conference because here the first attempt was made to fashion a permanent peace. The concept that a war might be fought to end war was a new one.

Wilson brought to Paris a document he called The Fourteen Points. It listed the major goals he hoped could be reached by the peacemakers at Versailles. When he returned to Washington only one goal had been achieved—the League of Nations, a precursor to the United Nations, which gasped for fifteen years, then folded under the onslaught of Hitler and Mussolini.

Should diplomats' personalities influence peace settlements?

It was Lloyd George, Orlando, and above all the French tiger Clemenceau (who had growled, "Fourteen points, why God Almighty had only Ten") who were most responsible for dashing Wilson's hopes for a permanent peace. Day after day, night after night, in the Hall of Mirrors and in Parisian hotels, the Big Three of Europe whittled away at the map of Europe and the Covenant of the League of Nations.

First they grabbed off the major overseas territories of Austria-Hungary and Germany. Then, to make sure that the Austro-Hungarian Empire would never again rise, they created the new states of Austria, Hungary, and from the tiny Balkan states where World War I began, Yugoslavia and Czechoslovakia. The principle of self-determination of various nationalities, a major point of Woodrow Wilson's, again and again went down to defeat before the Big Three.

One plea for self-determination that fell on deaf ears (even Wilson failed to learn of it) laid the basis for some of the major difficulties of the mid-twentieth century in Southeast Asia.

An obscure, youthful idealist from Indochina, working as a cook's assistant in hotels in Paris and London, joined with some similarly situated Southeast Asians living in Paris. In 1919 they drew up a petition for self-determination for the tiny jungle country of Vietnam. When the petition for freedom and independence for Vietnam was quietly brushed aside by the peacemakers in Paris, the cook's assistant conceded to his friends that his idea of a peaceful road to self-determination was unrealistic. In 1920 this young man, who later took the name Ho Chi Minh, became a co-founder of the French Communist Party.

The League of Nations was conceived by Wilson as a worldwide body comprising delegates from every nation, with particular weight given to the Big Four—Great Britain, France, Italy, and the United States. The League was to arbitrate and mediate international disputes before they mushroomed into major conflicts.

The League was hamstrung from the start. First, the United States never became a member. United States participation was opposed by a clique of isolationist senators, led by Henry Cabot Lodge of Massachusetts, who ultimately succeeded in killing the entire proposal. Any chance the League might have had to prohibit future wars was further trampled by the Big Three at Paris. They removed the provisions in the Covenant that provided for a standing military force and, in fact, banned any League action in disputes unless the disputing parties invited its intervention.

By 1928 many observers had conceded the failure of the League to accomplish anything but provide a forum for propaganda by the diplomats of the major powers. Nevertheless the idea of "peace in our time," first sounded by Wilson ten years before, had begun to take root throughout Europe and especially in the United States, whose citizens were concerned with protecting their isolation during the booming 1920s and fearful of a second European war into which they would inevitably be drawn.

Therefore, two diplomats, both pragmatists in contrast to the idealist Wilson, conceived a plan—a treaty to end war by outlawing it, by rendering it "illegal." United States Secretary of State Frank B. Kellogg and French Foreign Minister Aristide Briand were responsible for the authorship of the Kellogg-Briand Pact. On August 27, 1928, representatives of fifteen nations signed the agreement. It provided, first, that the "High Contracting Parties solemnly declare in the names of their respective peoples that they condemn recourse to war for the solution of international controversies, and renounce it as an instrument of national policy in their relations with one another."

Second, they agreed "that the settlement or solution of all disputes or conflicts of whatever nature or of whatever origin they may be, which may arise among them, shall never be sought except by pacific means."

The next year, 1929, Frank B. Kellogg was awarded the Nobel Peace Prize for his efforts. Six years later the troops of Benito Mussolini of Italy occupied Ethiopia, and in 1939 Hitler's blitzkrieg swept into Poland, forever burying the Kellogg-Briand Pact in the dustbin of history.

The failure of the Kellogg-Briand Pact and the similarly futile peacemaking efforts of the League of Nations did, however, have one important consequence. In 1941 when the Atlantic Charter delineating the Allied war aims was signed, and in 1942 when twenty-six nations signed the United Nations Declaration in Washington, the diplomats realized that, to make a permanent peace, it was not sufficient simply to express some ambitions in that direction.

Consequently, after extensive discussions among the Allies at Moscow, Washington, Yalta, and finally San Francisco, a United Nations was set up—this time with a Security Council having the power to invoke, first, economic and diplomatic sanctions and, finally, force against an aggressor.

Franklin Roosevelt and Winston Churchill realized, as Wilson, Lloyd George, Clemenceau, and Orlando had not, that a functioning United Nations was important to world security. Joseph Stalin, Russian chief of state, agreed to such a body in return for Allied military assistance. Thus, in 1945 in San Francisco, delegates from the major powers formed the United Nations. The next year Trygve Lie was elected secretary general in London.

I do not see any way of realizing our hopes about world organization in five or six days. Even the Almighty took seven.

Winston Churchill, 1944

In 1950 the United Nations faced the first international test of its mettle, and in its success proved that it had overcome the major faults of its League of Nations predecessor —weakness and inactivity. In that year, North Korean troops, backed by heavy military aid from neighboring Communist China, crossed the 38th parallel and invaded American-backed South Korea.

Within hours, an emergency session of the United Nations Security Council was called. The Soviet delegate had withdrawn from the Council several months before over the question of the admission of Communist China, so there was no opposition when the United States ambassador asked the United Nations to give its backing to the South Korean defense effort.

Should Communist China have been admitted to the UN in 1950?

American troops were already on their way into action when the Security Council announced the joint war aims of the United Nations. Diplomats at the time expressed hope that, although this was the first military action taken by a young body originally framed to keep peace, a show of force against blatant aggression would augur well for the future.

More than a year later, on July 10, 1951, United States Vice Admiral C. Turner Joy sat down in a bullet-marked former teahouse two miles south of the 38th parallel, faced Lieutenant General Nam Il, chief of staff of the North Korean army, and began talking peace. Two years after that, at 10 A.M. July 27, 1953, Admiral Joy's successor at the peace table, Lieutenant General William Harrison, Jr., began signing the first of nine copies of the armistice agreement. Twelve hours later the shooting stopped.

The Korean War was the first of the major *brushfire wars* that began in the post-World War II nuclear age. It was by far the largest until the outbreak of the expanded Vietnam War, and it was certainly the most comprehensive in terms of the number of nations committed to the hostilities.

The negotiations over Korea foreshadowed scores of other such talks held across the globe in the following years. Even officials at the Paris peace talks on the Vietnam War, fifteen years later, were haunted by the specter of the Korea negotiations, which dragged on for more than three years while 12,000 Americans died and 50,000 were wounded.

The grim obstinacy of the North Koreans, their unsmiling, unflagging energy to sit it out, made the negotiations difficult. They held to a firm and unyielding ideology—all of Korea should come under the Communist leader Kim Il Sung. At the same time they were convinced that the United States would not dare unleash the power of a nuclear device in such a limited conflict.

Finally, United Nations negotiators helped break the impasse at the peace table at Panmunjom. But today, along the border of barbed wire and watch towers that marks the line between North and South Korea, soldiers of the United Nations and North Korea walk their patrols. At Panmunjom, Communist and Western peace negotiators sit down periodically and review the "offenses" committed by each side. A truce was accomplished at Panmunjom, but not yet a real peace.

While the state exists there is no freedom; when there is freedom there will be no state.

Nikolai Lenin, 1917

Today a war of sorts still continues on a global scale; many call it "a war with no peace." On September 2, 1947, columnist Walter Lippmann, writing in the *New York Herald Tribune*, gave this war a name—a name that has stuck for twenty-five years. He called it the *cold war*.

It is a war whose series of peace efforts were closely affected by the personalities and characters of the leaders of the two major nations: Stalin, Roosevelt, and Truman; Khrushchev, Eisenhower, and Kennedy; Kosygin, Brezhnev, Johnson, and Nixon.

More than in any other twentieth century conflict, the eyeball-to-eyeball confrontation, whether in person or via intercontinental communication, has proved most crucial in cold war diplomacy and peacemaking. But often it has been the threat of nuclear power that proved equally important in tipping the balance in confrontation situations.

In January 1924 Nikolai Lenin, founder of the international Communist movement and the man most responsible for its first successful takeover of a nation, died. He had never met with a major Western leader, let alone a president of the United States. His only important peace attempt was a frantic effort to extricate his country from World War I, a war that had enabled him to effect the overthrow of the czar and the White Russians, but which, he feared, could also result in his own downfall. Therefore, on March 3, 1918, Lenin signed with the Germans the Treaty of Brest-Litovsk, stripping Russia of one-third its population. It was a humiliation Russia was not soon to forget—a humiliation that lasted in Soviet memory to the years after World War II.

For nine years after the death of Lenin, Russia was an exile from, or an alien to, the community of nations. Stalin, eventually to become the successor to Lenin, spent that time solidifying his power in the Kremlin.

At the same time, Stalin bolstered his hold over the foreign Communist parties—the nonruling parties that were to become allies, although occasionally thorns as well, in the cold war ahead.

Finally, in November 1933, the United States formally recognized Russia, and for the first time since its exclusion from the Paris Peace Conference of 1919, the Soviet Union was once again recognized as a first-class power. On September 17, 1934, the Soviets took their seat in the, by then, virtually powerless League of Nations.

Another decade passed, however, before the first major peace conferences between East and West convened. In the interim, in an effort to secure their borders and maintain a tenuous peace, the Soviet and Nazi foreign ministers concluded the Russo-German Nonaggression Pact of 1939.

This was a curious set of negotiaions. Although Molotov signed for the Soviets, Joseph Stalin took almost sole charge of the complex negotiations. It was his brutal, forceful personality imposed on the German Ribbentrop that was responsible for whatever concessions the Soviets were able to wring out of the Nazi war machine. Winning first a guarantee of Russia's borders against German aggression, Stalin then persuaded Ribbentrop to yield Finland to the Soviet sphere of influence.

All of these maneuverings between the Soviets and Nazis were to have a profound impact on the West. Here was a Communist totalitarian state, already suspect for Lenin's pronouncements that Communism would rule the world, apparently dividing the spoils of Europe with the world's other major totalitarian state. The four-month war of conquest the Soviets waged against Finland did little to improve the Soviets' image as a peace loving power.

When it became increasingly evident that Germany was itching for any excuse to violate the Nonaggression Pact and launch into the Soviet Union, however, Stalin began to send out peace feelers to the West. Diplomats in Washington and Moscow consistently urged their leaders to action. But in the end, it was Franklin Roosevelt and Joseph Stalin who concluded the wartime truce that temporarily suspended the cold war.

By autumn of 1943 the Soviet Union and the United States, together with the rest of the major wartime Allies, were themselves dividing the spoils of the peace. Woodrow Wilson's concept of "peace without victory" was scarcely considered as Stalin, Roosevelt, and Churchill met in Teheran, Iran, and began to draw up the blueprints of postwar Europe and the United Nations. In Teheran, Roosevelt and Stalin met face-to-face for the first time.

Roosevelt was an optimist. If he had any failing in these peace talks it was in underestimating the extreme callousness of his opponent. If we just talk reasonably and rationally with him and exhibit friendship, Roosevelt told his advisers, perhaps Stalin will meet us halfway.

Should Roosevelt have trusted Stalin?

In the opening sessions Stalin was all beaming joy. He proposed toasts to his visitors, conceded the establishment of a United Nations, and helped plot a joint military operation in Europe. But when it came down to the security of the Soviet Union, Stalin was obstinate. It has always been the objective of Russian diplomacy that in whatever peace is made, the nation must expand in order to remain secure. Therefore, the czars added the vast Asian area of Siberia, Lenin expanded into the Baltic region, and Stalin sought to preserve Eastern Europe for the new Soviet State. At Teheran, even while a truce was in effect, the seeds of the renewed cold war were planted.

There was a succession of Allied peace conferences while the war against the Axis continued. In each, Stalin or Molotov gave small sops to the West, and the West continued to make the compromises that resulted in the presence of American troops in Western Europe twenty-five years after World War II.

17

At Yalta, in the Soviet Crimea, where Stalin hosted his Western guests in the spas of the Black Sea resort, the Soviets finally gave in on the United Nations question, an issue Roosevelt had considered resolved earlier at Teheran. In return, the United States virtually gave Poland to the Soviet Union by promising not to interfere with Soviet efforts to set up a puppet government in exile. Poland was the first Soviet toehold in Eastern Europe.

Stalin had agreed in utmost friendship to virtually everything at Teheran, Yalta, and then Potsdam. But upon returning to the red brick walls of the Kremlin in Moscow, he sent out messages reneging on the agreements—second thoughts, he called them. He procrastinated in agreeing to grant the major powers a veto in the United Nations and, meanwhile, refused to guarantee the sanctity of free governments in Eastern Europe. Stalin, friendly as long as he needed Western military aid to keep the Germans at bay, retired into coldness and reserve. The tenuous wartime peace between East and West was severed when Soviet tanks rolled through Eastern Europe into Germany.

By the summer of 1946, Communist cadres were spreading guerrilla warfare throughout Greece, and Communist operatives were moving into independent Czechoslovakia, preparing for a bloody coup there. On March 5, 1946, the peace he had so carefully nurtured collapsing around him and his government in serious political trouble, Britain's Winston Churchill, addressing a special convocation at Fulton, Missouri, proclaimed, "From Stettin in the Baltic to Trieste in the Adriatic, an iron curtain has descended across the Continent."

A year later, President Truman made the final gesture to his former ally by inviting the war-ravaged Soviet Union to join the Marshall Plan and receive United States aid. In an impassioned speech in Paris, however, Soviet Foreign Minister Molotov rejected the offer.

No peace treaty between the Allied and Axis powers was signed following World War II, so Germany became the next battleground of the cold war. For twenty-five years that country was to be the focus of peace wranglings, diplomatic maneuverings, intrigues, and frustrations of the undeclared war between East and West.

From 1945 to 1949 there were a series of conferences of the allied Council of Foreign Ministers, aimed at forming a peace to end the war. Generally, the conferences ended in petty bickering between the principals. Molotov, a brilliant tactician, had little room to maneuver, since Stalin was constantly breathing fire down his neck. Secretary of State James F. Byrnes and his two successors under Truman, George C. Marshall and Dean Acheson, while able administrators and brilliant diplomats, faced strong pressure from the increasingly vocal right wing in the United States. As Truman gained confidence, he too wanted to exert a stronger influence in diplomacy and peacemaking.

The pattern of postwar peacemaking began to emerge—a pattern that was to be repeated again and again from Vietnam to the Middle East, from Cyprus to Nigeria. The professional diplomats, the secretaries of state, the foreign ministers, and the ambassadors were increasingly hampered by heads of state who made their own foreign policies, leaving the professionals powerless to negotiate. The cold war, whether focused on Europe, the Middle East, or the Far East, reflected the national leaders' ideological differences.

Are professional diplomats better qualified to make peace than heads of state?

Through the 1950s the Soviets continually proposed summit conferences, only to cancel them angrily weeks or even days later with an outraged burst of propaganda. The Soviets' detonation of their first nuclear device in 1949 only increased their intransigence.

On March 5, 1953, Joseph Stalin, while vacationing at his retreat in the Crimea, died after suffering a cerebral hemorrhage. With his death ended an era in which a decision of a single head of the Soviet state could dramatically reverse the course of Russian foreign policy. It was several years before Nikita Khrushchev was able to consolidate his rule completely. But it was a rule unlike any other Russia had ever seen. Khrushchev was a showman par excellence.

He was garrulous, at times lugubrious, temperamental, and always unpredictable. He alternated between threats and smiles at the peace tables he frequented from New York to Vienna, from Peking to Jakarta. And he provoked and made the peaces that followed the innumerable skirmishes and conflicts of the cold war.

As he began to assert his power, Khrushchev established his doctrine of personal diplomacy. In May 1955 he traveled to Belgrade and made a personal gesture of peace to Yugoslavia's Tito. India's Jawaharlal Nehru and Germany's Konrad Adenauer led a parade of heads of state through the gates of the Kremlin to sit by Khrushchev's side and listen to his pleas for peaceful coexistence, which was to replace the Stalinist policy of pressure on every front.

But it was Khrushchev's character that more than any other single factor determined the course of peacemaking in the fifties and into the sixties. In 1958 he was menacing West Berlin, applying pressure at one of the West's most sensitive areas. The next year he was smiling his way across the United States under the invitation of President Eisenhower. But the relaxation of tensions achieved at the Camp David talks evaporated the following May when his first major summit conference was scheduled to begin in Paris.

On May 1, 1960, an American U–2 reconnaissance plane was shot down inside the Soviet Union. President Eisenhower was already in Paris awaiting the arrival of the Soviet leader, as were Britain's Prime Minister Macmillan and France's President de Gaulle. Khrushchev reacted truculently. He threatened retaliation by Soviet missiles against any nation that allowed Western planes to take off for flights over Russia, then broke off the conference.

That autumn, world relations still strained over the failure of the two major powers to meet across the peace table, Khrushchev made a grand appearance at the United Nations, but he set few fears to rest. He held impromptu shirt-sleeve press conferences, harangued his colleagues, and when a member of the General Assembly began a speech he did not care for, he removed his shoe and pounded his desk.

In this atmosphere, John F. Kennedy took over the reins of United States diplomacy in January 1961. The freeze in Soviet-American relations had solidified in the previous eight months. The United States supported invasion of Cuba by

*We cannot
negotiate with
those who say,
"What's mine is
mine and what's
yours is
negotiable."*

John F. Kennedy, 1961

anti-Castro exiles did not improve relations. After a few perfunctory gestures by the Soviets toward the new president, including the freeing of two American airmen who had been seized when their reconnaissance plane was shot down in July 1960 off northern Russia, the stage was set for a face-to-face confrontation between the two world leaders.

Khrushchev sought to test the mettle of his new young adversary. They were from decidedly different backgrounds: the Soviet leader was from a peasant family in the rural area of Russia's Ukraine, reared in poverty, promoted to leadership through an uphill battle of political intrigues, death, and brutality. The American president was young, aristocratic, scion of one of the wealthiest families in the world, and had risen to power in a series of seemingly effortless, quick, and brilliant moves.

Khrushchev was impressed as the two men sank into the leather-covered chairs in the Vienna conference room in June 1961. But outward amicability proved of little help in establishing a working peace between their countries. The two leaders remained sharply divided on the issues of access to Berlin and a nuclear test ban, although they agreed on a "neutral and independent Laos."

Nevertheless, within two months, the Soviets announced a resumption of nuclear testing. And a year later (1962) President Kennedy confronted the Soviet leader with the presence of Soviet-supplied missiles in Cuba. The Cuban Missile Crisis was an "eyeball-to-eyeball confrontation, and Khrushchev blinked," said one observer at the time. President Kennedy acknowledged later how close the crisis had brought the world to nuclear holocaust. But it was a testimony to the new diplomacy of the 1960s that a settlement was reached without a conference table.

The Russian missiles were withdrawn, and Khrushchev suffered a permanent loss of prestige; in 1964 he was forced into retirement. In the next eight years the course of the cold war changed only slightly. The leadership of Brezhnev and Kosygin displayed none of the flamboyance of Khrushchev, and equally none of the penchant for talk and barter. They were busy with their own internal problems, with the growing menace from Peking, and with delicate political problems in their East European satellites.

It was not, in fact, until 1969 that the next major East-West peace conference convened in Helsinki and later in Vienna. This series of negotiations between the United States and the Soviet Union acquired the name SALT talks, an acronym for Strategic Arms Limitation Talks. Moving from Helsinki to Vienna and back, the talks, as announced in October 1969, were to discuss limitations on the superpowers' vast nuclear missile arsenals.

On November 17, 1969, diplomats Gerard C. Smith of the United States and Vladimir S. Semyonov of the Soviet Union gathered in the ornate Finnish state banquet hall in Helsinki and pledged to avoid putting the other side at any disadvantage. President Nixon sent a message to the opening meeting, and foreign affairs experts in the two world capitals kept a close watch on the progress of the top-secret negotiating sessions.

Why were the SALT talks conducted in secret?

Preliminary sessions gave way to full negotiating sessions, and the guidelines for the talks were worked out. Finally, in May 1972, President Nixon, while on a state visit to the Soviet Union, and General Secretary Brezhnev signed two documents which had been hammered out in the SALT discussions. One was an ABM treaty limiting each side's defensive missile systems. The other was an interim agreement—to last five years—which placed ceilings on the production of offensive weapons. In addition, both nations pledged to continue the SALT talks in order to work out further agreements.

At the beginning, the outlook for meaningful negotiations at SALT was gloomy. After all, both nations were involved on opposite sides in an undeclared war, and the tensions over Vietnam were bound to influence the progress of the talks. Yet, paradoxically, the United States and the Soviet Union agreed to a cutback in their armaments, while Vietnam remained an unresolved conflict. Perhaps this paradox can be explained by a closer look at the problem in Southeast Asia.

A people who have courageously opposed French domination for more than eighty years, a people who have fought side by side with the Allies against the Fascists during these last years, such a people must be free and independent.

Ho Chi Minh, 1945

For more than two thousand years the Asian territory called Indochina and more specifically Vietnam has known the swords of invaders and the rule of foreign hands. For nearly one thousand years, the Chinese helped themselves to the rich resources of this protrusion on the Asian mainland. For another seven centuries the Indochinese struggled among themselves; the Vietnamese, the Khmers, and the Chams seesawed back and forth for control of the rice-rich lowlands of the peninsula.

In 1627, the French missionary priest Monsignor Alexandre de Rhodes first landed on the Indochinese mainland. Two centuries passed, however, before the French government realized the potential of this unclaimed corner of the Asian continent and landed military forces in Vietnam.

During most of the French occupation of Indochina (from 1858–1954) there were no attempts at peacemaking. Like most Western colonial governments, the French simply moved in and took over. They set up factories, schools, and administrative networks. There was, in truth, no real power with which the French could negotiate until the Japanese occupied Indochina during World War II. And then suddenly there were too many: first the Japanese; then the emperor, Bao Dai; then the new nationalists led by Ho Chi Minh.

Ho Chi Minh instigated the first real efforts at peace, and, as an immediate corollary, the first real armed conflict with the French in Indochina and Vietnam. On September 2,

Are colonial
governments always
exploitative?

1945, Ho stood on the balcony of the Hanoi Opera House and proclaimed to the throngs in the street the establishment of the Democratic Republic of Vietnam, the second Communist state in Asia. Within days, the French realized that they would have to negotiate with this man.

Ho Chi Minh was born in 1890. The son of a local civil servant, he became the only major head of government to play a key role in every Indochina peace talk of the twentieth century. As Nguyen Ai Quoc (one of the names he used prior to his adoption of the name Ho Chi Minh late in life) he was first rebuffed in his efforts to achieve an independent Vietnam while at the Paris Peace Conference in 1919 (see p. 9). Ho became a dedicated Communist. A co-founder of the French Communist Party, he served on the Comintern (Communist International) in Moscow and later in the Far East. Finally, on May 19, 1941, he reappeared at Pac Bo in the northernmost tip of Vietnam to form the Communist-dominated Vietminh. Then in the first months of 1946, Ho and his close personal friend, the permanent French representative Jean Sainteny, negotiated and signed an accord recognizing the Democratic Republic of Vietnam. It was a short-lived peace.

These first Vietnam peace talks took place in an atmosphere of rare good will during those halcyon days after the Japanese had been driven off. But cordiality evaporated quickly as Ho and his aides waited in the French Colonial Office in Paris in July and August to formalize the agreement recognizing the continued French presence in Vietnam. On September 14, 1946, an accord of sorts was signed by Ho and the French overseas minister, Marius Moutet.

Three months later, on December 19, 1946, the accord, already a shambles due to French impatience, large-scale troop movements, and colossal misunderstandings on all sides, was shattered. On that day French and Communist troops began a war that was to end eight years and hundreds of thousands of casualties later.

On April 26, 1954, the long black limousines belonging to diplomats from the United States, France, Britain, the Soviet Union, and Communist China drew up to the entrance of the Palais des Nations in Geneva, where twenty years before the expiring League of Nations had breathed its last. Thousands of miles to the east, French troops had their backs to the wall at Dien Bien Phu.

The Communists sent to Geneva the two giants of their diplomatic community—Soviet Foreign Minister Vyacheslav Molotov and Chinese Foreign Minister Chou En-lai. They held all the cards—Communist control of large populated areas of Vietnam, a tough strategic force, and opponents who were anxious to rid themselves of an unprofitable and distasteful war.

Both Molotov and Chou were veteran negotiators. Chou was, in addition, a product of the terrifying Long March (1934–1935), a 6,000-mile journey during which the Chinese Communists were pursued by the Nationalist army of Chiang Kai-shek. Chou had known the privations of the guerrilla fighter. And, from countless negotiations with the Kuomintang (Chinese Nationalists) and the Western powers, he knew the ways of diplomacy.

Molotov too was a proven negotiator. Although he had little first-hand knowledge of the hardships of a jungle war, he knew the value of bargaining from a strong strategic position and of a peaceful image in dealing with the West.

The Western side, in contrast, was confused, divided, and composed of a constantly changing kaleidoscope of negotiators having varying degrees of power and responsibility. Initially, the Western delegations were headed by Secretary of State John Foster Dulles of the United States and Foreign Minister Georges Bidault of France. But soon Dulles flew home, and Bidault became preoccupied with the severe domestic problems facing his own government in Paris.

The talks dragged on in Geneva through May and June and into a sweltering July. Dulles announced the final terms of the settlement at a Washington news conference on July 23, 1954. He summed up the problem in one sentence: "After nearly eight years of war, the forces of the French Union had lost control of nearly one-half of Vietnam, their hold on the balance was precarious, and the French people did not desire to prolong the war."

There was more at stake at Geneva, however, than a small peninsula on the tip of the Chinese mainland. At stake was the entire South Asian subcontinent, and, if Dulles's *domino theory* (that successive countries would fall to Communist domination) was correct, the future of the entire Far East hung in the balance.

Therefore, the solution reached at Geneva played a crucial role in peacemaking efforts over the next two decades. It provided what was then looked upon as a workable solution to an insoluble problem: how to give the native Communists what they had in fact won on the battlefield—namely the country and people of Vietnam—while still preserving a semblance of neutrality for that part of Asia.

The French had proposed a collection of troops on both sides in assigned strategic areas, followed by national elections supervised by a commission of neutral nations; in Laos and Cambodia, withdrawal of all Communist forces; and a guarantee of these terms by the Geneva powers.

The Communists, nominally headed by the Vietminh, since it was after all their country over whom everyone was negotiating a peace, had proposed the collection of troops and elections supervised by commissions formed from the Vietnam and Vietminh regimes, rather than by neutrals (as the French and the West desired). They proposed the same solution in Laos and Cambodia—in other words, no Communist troop withdrawals—and called for total withdrawal of all French troops from Indochina before the elections.

Given these differing terms, the fact that an agreement was reached is a tribute to the negotiators, as well as evidence of the desperate need for peace. The Russians, for instance, wanted peace on their eastern border. They were worried about Berlin and the East-West German situation and power struggles within the Soviet Union. The Chinese, faced with a stalemate in Korea at Panmunjom, wanted no additional difficulties with the Vietminh.

The final document, however, was a victory more for the Communists than for any power in the West. It might have been considered a diplomatic defeat for the United States except for one fact—the United States never signed it.

The actual treaty text provided for two Vietnams—North and South—divided at the 17th parallel. The North was to be controlled entirely by the Vietminh, the South by the French, until an independent election resulting in reunification could be held in both sectors.

In his Washington news conference, Dulles, a hardline anti-Communist and crusty negotiator who often vowed never to give an inch to the "Red peril," asserted that since the settlements contained "many features which we do not like" and since "the United States itself was neither a belligerent in Indochina nor subject to compulsions which applied to others, we did not become a party of the conference results."

Nguyen Thanh Le, a member of the 1954 Vietminh delegation, occupied a back seat during the Geneva conference. Fourteen years later he was a senior member of the North Vietnamese delegation to the 1968–1972 Paris peace talks on the Vietnam War. From his viewpoint, the war between North and South Vietnam was caused by a United States sabotage of the Geneva Agreement. In a 1970 interview, Le said, "When the Geneva conference on Vietnam started, Mr. Dulles left Geneva and left behind Mr. Bedell Smith, who was at that time Assistant Secretary of State. Thus, the United States downgraded the governments of the 1954 Geneva conference. . . . [Also] the United States did not sign the Geneva Agreement, while the other participants signed it."

Should the U.S. have signed the Geneva Accords?

The Vietminh felt they had been laughed at and sneered at in Geneva in 1954. The spoils of their victory over the French had been snatched from them by their Russian and Chinese allies. They had won only half of the country to which they were entitled—they had lost the other half not on the battlefield but at the peace table. This would not happen again, they vowed.

Our objective is the independence of South Vietnam and its freedom from attack. We want nothing for ourselves—only that the people of South Vietnam be allowed to guide their own country in their own way.

Lyndon B. Johnson, 1965

Fourteen years passed before the Vietnamese Communists and the Americans again sat down together in an effort to resolve their differences. If someone had told the peace-makers who walked out of the Palais des Nations in Geneva in July 1954 that it was to be fourteen years of little peace and more bloodshed than that tiny peninsula had ever known, the news probably would have been greeted by a shrug of quiet resignation. For the peace that was charted that hot summer day was never to be. The treaty provisions were broken almost as soon as the ink was dry.

The signatories of the 1954 Geneva Accords did not intend for Vietnam to be perpetually divided. They envisioned in some future time a single Vietnam, quite possibly Communist but nevertheless one that determined its own fate. The Vietminh in the North were willing to wait for what they saw as an inevitable historical imperative.

The accords provided that in July 1956 there would be a general election throughout Vietnam to elect a unity government. A control commission of representatives of the North and the South was set up to enable communication between the two sectors. But by 1956 the outlines of the destruction of the Geneva Accords were already apparent. President Ngo Dinh Diem of South Vietnam scrapped the unity election with the offhand statement that the security situation in the South would not permit it. In May 1958 Diem dissolved the control commission, his sole link with the North, and expelled the North Vietnamese Communists who staffed it.

It took four years for a shooting war to break out again in the South. In the meantime, the North Vietnamese organized a complex system of political and military cadres, built their supply routes, and began their needling attacks, which grew increasingly more provocative and dangerous to the Diem regime. By 1962 the United States was heavily committed to the support of South Vietnam, both militarily and politically, and large numbers of American "advisers" poured into the country. By the spring of 1965 when the first marines landed at Da Nang and the first air mission was flown over Vinh Linh, the United States was at war.

Why did the American people allow U.S. participation in an undeclared war?

Now, when American diplomats finally reacted to the fact that there was a war in Southeast Asia, the first moves toward a peace began. Between 1965 and 1967 there were at least forty-five separate fully documented peace feelers and countless other diplomatic niceties exchanged between the principals. For a new kind of peace was sought—a peace for a war that, officially at least, did not exist. The Geneva truce had never been abrogated. War had never been declared. The Communists did not intend to come to a peace table and, as they had in Geneva, lose what they had won on the battlefield. And the Americans, unlike the French, never acknowledged that they had an enemy with whom they could negotiate.

The principals in this delicate pas de deux did their dance in the world capitals—in Washington and Moscow and Hanoi. The teletype was their peace table and their negotiators were heads of state. The diplomats were the errand boys. There were no "open covenants, openly arrived at," as President Wilson desired in 1919, but secret covenants, secretly arrived at.

There were, then, two phases in the current Vietnam peace talks, much as in the war itself—the "undeclared" and the "declared." The undeclared phase was from 1965 through 1968, when both sides professed a great desire to meet but nothing happened. In the declared phase, from 1968 to 1973, representatives of the two belligerents confronted each other in an avowed effort to reach a peace—although for five years no peace was forthcoming.

Throughout the administration of Lyndon Johnson there were attempts on the part of the United States to reach some accommodation with the leaders in Hanoi, particularly with Ho Chi Minh, that could lead to talks. The war was in a critical phase. The United States applied pressure through increasingly heavy bombing raids against the heartland of North Vietnam and continued to pour manpower into enemy strongholds in the South. Both nations' leaders were proven negotiators, Lyndon Johnson through his years in the United States Congress, Ho Chi Minh through his years at countless peace tables, East and West.

President Johnson did not want to lose face. By the middle of his administration the war was known in some circles as "Johnson's War," and he did not want history to record that he was the first president to lead America to defeat on the battlefield or at a peace table. Ho did not want to repeat the mistakes that led to what he considered a defeat in 1954.

There were various pipelines through which "unofficial" talks were kept open. U Thant, secretary general of the United Nations, in the course of his travels throughout the world and his talks with countless diplomats in New York, endeavored to bring both sides toward some agreement. There were other various intermediaries who traveled to Hanoi, met in back conference rooms in a dozen world capitals, and exchanged *feelers*—the polite diplomatic word for hesitant conversations that may precede a full-scale peace conference. But President Johnson's decision not to run for a second term and to cease bombing North Vietnam brought the leaders of both countries within ideological handshaking distance. Finally, in April 1968, the word came from Hanoi: Ho Chi Minh's negotiators would meet an American team in Paris to discuss terms for talks.

"They [the North Vietnamese] felt that with the Tet offensive [in January 1968] they had thrown LBJ out of office," said a senior State Department diplomat. "The purpose of the talks from their point of view was simply to spell out the terms of surrender. They thought they had the war won. But the dickering that resulted was a total disillusionment. That's when the propaganda set in."

What were the U.S.
objectives at the
Paris talks?

When both sides assembled in Paris in May 1968, W. Averell Harriman of the United States faced off against Xuan Thuy of North Vietnam. At that point, each honestly expected a settlement to result. Both knew the background of the problem—they were familiar with the 1954 Geneva Accords—and as professional, veteran negotiators they trusted that a final peace for Southeast Asia could be fashioned. Mr. Harriman was the scion of a wealthy New York family, and he had held more government and diplomatic positions in the previous thirty-five years than most presidents of the United States. At seventy-six years of age, he was perhaps the only American diplomat with sufficient total prestige to carry a settlement in Paris to fruition in his own right.

His opponent was Xuan Thuy, former foreign minister of North Vietnam and known throughout the Communist world as his country's foremost diplomatic spokesman. A generation younger than his American counterpart, he was nevertheless a militant propagandist and an agile Communist theoretician.

The two had met before—in Geneva in 1961–1962 when for fifteen wearying months they had exchanged bombast and bargaining counters over the future of Laos. Each knew the other as a diplomat with staying power, although from the start of the 1968 talks, Xuan Thuy expected to be dictating the terms of a victory.

The initial months, indeed nearly the entire first year of the conference, showed Xuan Thuy that he had misjudged the situation. The "preliminary conversations" dragged on and on. Were the "full talks" to include two or four delegations? What was to be the shape of the table? The speaking order? The protocol? The agenda? High level diplomatic debate degenerated to petty wrangling over the shape of the conference table until January 18, 1969, when the impasse was broken. A circular table was hastily constructed by the hosting French government, and on January 25 the four delegations, now with a new chief American representative, Henry Cabot Lodge, sat down together to try to settle the war. But negotiating went very, very slowly.

"Do we take the talks seriously?" a senior American delegation spokesman in Paris was asked two and one-half years after the start of the negotiations.

"We take them deadly seriously," he replied. "There's nothing—no aspect of U.S. foreign policy, I guess, that is more serious than our problem in Southeast Asia, and the preferred way of solving it, as the president [Nixon] has said in every major speech that he's made on the subject, is through negotiations, if possible. It takes two to negotiate. It takes two to compromise. So where you run into utter intransigence, refusal to even begin the process of negotiation by the imposition of preconditions to the beginning of that process . . . [amounts] to the ceding to the other side of everything they ask for."

A questioner asked, "Then there hasn't been any progress in the twenty-two months since they decided on the shape of the conference table?"

"That's essentially correct," the United States diplomat responded.

What progress there was, in fact, took place thousands of miles from Paris—in the United States through televised presidential pronouncements, and through declarations formed in Hanoi and read from closely typed papers in Paris.

The talks stalemated on several major issues—the presence of American military personnel and North Vietnamese forces, the status of prisoners of war, and the nature of the postwar government of South Vietnam. Each side presented several peace programs couched in a number of "points," each point offering a solution to one of the issues. Between 1969 and 1971, the Communists proposed seven-point, eight-point, and ten-point plans. The United States offered a five-point and an eight-point plan. But no matter how many points were included or how many plans were proposed, none was found acceptable to the opposition.

For both sides, the peace talks were exercises not only in futility, but in propaganda as well. As soon as it became apparent that a quick end to the talks and the war was unlikely, as soon as it became apparent that neither side was about to gain a quick military advantage on the battlefields,

We cannot expect to make everyone our friend,
but we can try to make no one our enemy.

Richard M. Nixon, 1969

the chances of a real peace in Paris evaporated. Instead, the weekly sessions in the ornate ballroom of the Hotel Majestic became an effort to turn the tide of war by influencing the people who support the governments of each side. "We want to show the skeptical American how unwilling the other side is to bargain in good faith," said an American diplomat candidly.

While the public talks degenerated, "secret negotiations" were conducted by Henry Kissinger, President Nixon's special adviser for national security affairs, on the one side, and Xuan Thuy and representatives of the North Vietnamese on the other.

These top peacemakers met twelve times between 1969 and 1971, unbeknownst to the outside world, in small "safe," or secret, houses in and around Paris. Kissinger was the president's errand boy. By his own admission, he brought with him a series of peace plans, including eventual withdrawal of all American troops in exchange for the release of prisoners of war, and a political settlement determined by the Vietnamese people in a free election to be held after the resignation of the Saigon government.

Should major powers set peace conditions for smaller nations?

Kissinger and the president claimed the proposals were rejected immediately. The North Vietnamese claimed there had been no bargaining—the proposals were presented as an ultimatum. When North Vietnam offered its own plan, it was rejected by the United States.

Kissinger met in private talks with the North Vietnamese several times in 1972, and the negotiating pattern remained unbroken. The players changed—Kissinger was in for Harriman and Bruce. But the game was the same. Kissinger's power derived, not from his negotiating efforts in Paris, but from the influence of his advice on the president, an influence none of the other Paris negotiators possessed to the same extent.

By October 1972 it was obvious to most observers that the public series of weekly talks had failed in their announced mission. Only the personal contacts between Henry Kissinger and his North Vietnamese counterpart, Le Duc Tho, could hope to produce a peace. And though there was a false start and stop three weeks before the 1972 presidential election when Kissinger announced that peace was "at hand," the complex secret negotiations resulted in an agreement early the next year.

"It is obvious," Kissinger told members of the press on January 24, 1973, when he presented the text of the agreement and protocols ending the longest war in the nation's history, "that a war that has lasted for ten years will have many elements that cannot be completely satisfactory to all the parties concerned. . . . The North Vietnamese were working with dedication and seriousness on a conclusion—[during] the period in October and the period after we resumed the talks January 8. It was always clear that a lasting peace could come about only if neither side sought to achieve everything that it had wanted."

Why did secret talks rather than the public negotiations produce results?

Within weeks after the agreement was signed in Paris, the first American prisoners began returning from North Vietnam. The four-party truce observer teams and the four-nation mediation teams assumed their positions. Yet, was the war over?

The shooting had officially stopped. But skirmishes continued, and the truce teams were frequently fired upon and harassed. The official negotiators had called the agreement signed in Paris, "Agreement on Ending the War and Restoring Peace in Vietnam." *The New York Times* in publishing the text called it, "The Cease-Fire Agreement."

Who was correct? Both in a sense. If peace is defined as an end to the shooting, an exchange of prisoners of war, a return to the status quo ante bellum (the conditions that prevailed before the shooting began), then a peace treaty was concluded in Paris. But this was not the kind of peace Woodrow Wilson negotiated in 1919.

It is doubtful, given the clash of ideologies, the uncompromising nature of the bargainers on both sides, and above all the indecisive conclusion on the battlefields, that Henry Kissinger could have played the role of a Woodrow Wilson —nor for that matter could President Nixon himself. The nature of the talks, as the nature of the two wars, were poles apart.

For one thing, Wilson was his own negotiator. As president, he could dictate his own terms, make his own deals, act as his own diplomat. The ambassadors at the most recent Paris talks were mouthpieces. Teletypes linked the Paris embassies with the foreign ministries and the heads of state. Policy decisions were made on the basis of long-range military-diplomatic planning, domestic political considerations, and the exigencies of the cold war.

A settlement of the Vietnam War may have been signed in the French capital, but it was reached in other world capitals, irrespective of any diplomatic niceties around a conference table.

*The victories that
we have won have
never intoxicated
us or filled us with
such complacency
as to relinquish
the wish and call
for peace—a
peace that means
good neighborly
relations,
cooperation and an
end to slaughter.*

Golda Meir, 1970

Chapter Five The UN and the Middle East

Early on the morning of May 14, 1948, the Israeli state radio broadcast the Jewish hymn "Ha-Tikvah" and proclaimed the establishment of a new nation—the Jewish state of Israel. Within hours, the combined armies of the Arab states, poised on the frontiers of the new country, invaded, setting off the first of three brief bloody wars that punctuated the third quarter of the twentieth century in the Middle East.

It is ironic that the state of Israel and the first Middle East war began almost simultaneously with the creation of the United Nations—the organization that since then has tried to arrange and enforce peace.

Quickly convening in an emergency session as soon as the combined armies of Egypt, Jordan, Iraq, Lebanon, and Syria crossed into Israel, the United Nations Security Council sent two of its most respected peacemakers to the Middle East—Count Folke Bernadotte of Sweden and Dr. Ralph J. Bunche of the United States. By September 17, 1948, Count Bernadotte lay dead, the victim of assassins, and the task of arranging a peace fell to Dr. Bunche.

Dr. Bunche faced a curious situation as he flew to the Greek Island of Rhodes in the Mediterranean Sea, a reasonably neutral ground, and assembled representatives of the various sides around him. None of the Arab representatives even recognized the existence of their principal belligerent, Israel. And Israel, adrift in a sea of enemies, wanted only a guarantee of its continued existence. So Dr. Bunche evolved a unique method of peacemaking—a method that acquired

41

the name *the Rhodes Formula* and served as a prototype for future peacemaking efforts in the Middle East and elsewhere.

Shortly after the first of January 1949, with the Middle East in a tense state of truce, the various delegations assembled at Rhodes. Dr. Bunche was the sole party truly interested in a peace. The delegations met in separate rooms; Dr. Bunche shuttled back and forth, trading compromises, smoothing ruffled tempers, and at some points keeping the belligerent diplomats from one another's throats. Then both sides were brought together as the talks grew to a climax.

"We made up the rules as we went along," Dr. Bunche said, describing his method of bargaining. As each side arrived, Dr. Bunche called on the leading members separately in order to determine what kind of agenda to draw up.

The next step was a joint meeting for the purpose of approving the agenda and signing a cease-fire accord. "There was a double purpose in this," he later told an interviewer. "Primarily, it was to get both sides to meet—but also, I wanted them both to get accustomed to taking formal action, and to signing something. That way, I figured, the next step might not be so difficult."

But, in fact, every step was tedious, frustrating work. There were countless petty diplomatic problems. The Jordanian delegate refused to shake hands with the Israeli until it was explained that it was not a fact of recognition of the state of Israel but simply a polite, gentlemanly courtesy. At one point, in a moment of pique, the Israeli delegate slammed his pencil to the table; it ricocheted, striking the Egyptian envoy. Dr. Bunche refused to resume the meeting until the Egyptian had received an apology.

Finally, forty-two days after the first delegate had stepped off the plane on Rhodes, an armistice agreement was reached. In large part it was a tribute to the moral force of world opinion as expressed through the United Nations. Time after time, Dr. Bunche used this bargaining counter as the last resort when the talks threatened to break up. On the other hand, the armistice was a recognition of the fact that the Israelis were the victors on the battlefield; the Arab armies lay in ruin.

How much does world opinion influence peace negotiations?

42

By July 20, 1949, the last of the bilateral armistice agreements was signed, and officially the Middle East was at peace. But an armistice agreement is not a peace treaty—not in the sense of the Versailles Treaty of 1919 or the Geneva Accords of 1954. It did not guarantee the winner the spoils of victory nor the vanquished the true humility of defeat. It did not require either side to recognize the victory or even the existence of the other. It merely provided that both sides would lay down their arms and stop shooting.

The 1949 agreements provided that all parties recognize the United Nations as the guarantor of the peace. But the armistice did not include adjustments of postwar boundaries, an agreement on the status of refugees, nor settlement of the question of navigation of nearby waters (including the Suez Canal)—all of which became issues in later peace conferences. Throughout the next seven years, the United Nations Conciliation Commission tried without success to arrange a peace treaty but failed even to arrange a conference. And within seven years, the area again flared into open warfare.

The 1956 war began over the unsettled problem of navigation through the Suez Canal. (In the history of peace conferences in the twentieth century, it has generally been the issues left unsettled that were responsible for the next conflict.) A more basic issue, however, in 1956, was also left over from 1949—Israel still existed and the Arab powers still wanted it destroyed.

The 1956 war was shorter and even bloodier than the 1949 one, and the Arab armies were more thoroughly destroyed. The armistice ending it (still no peace) lasted longer this time, however. The United Nations was again the guarantor and the peacemaker. In fact, the real peacemaker in this second round of negotiations was the United Nations Security Council and the peacekeeping force it created—the United Nations Emergency Force (UNEF) composed of troops of several neutral nations.

The peace conferences affecting the Middle East are typical of the new style of peace conference in the twentieth century. Certainly there were negotiators involved—lower-level diplomats from each of the concerned countries and

*Fate does not jest and events are not a matter of
chance—there is no existence out of nothing. We
cannot look at the map of the world without
seeing our own place upon it, and that our role
is dictated by that place.*

Gamal Abdul Nasser, 1955

numerous members of the professional staff of the United Nations. But the real peacemakers, the heads of state— Nasser of Egypt, Ben-Gurion of Israel, Hussein of Jordan, or Feisal of Saudi Arabia—held back. Each was responsible to popular sentiment in his country, and the peace terms demanded by each nation's people were incapable of being negotiated. Because the heads of state did not directly intervene in peacemaking, no effective negotiating was accomplished. For the next eleven years, blue-helmeted members of the United Nations Emergency Force presided over the area.

How do today's peace conferences differ from earlier ones?

The issues were left unsettled. There was no peace treaty; perhaps another war was inevitable. On the morning of June 5, 1967, Israeli jets flew low out of the desert, across the Sinai Peninsula, and in lightning attacks destroyed virtually the entire Soviet-supplied Egyptian air force. Israeli ground units swept through the Sinai Peninsula, across the Jordanian frontier, and onto the Golan Heights of Syria. Within six days, while the United Nations Security Council went into frantic around-the-clock emergency sessions, the war was over. And again, Israel had won on the battlefields.

At the peace tables, too, the earlier scenario was repeated. Secretary General U Thant appointed Swedish diplomat Gunnar V. Jarring mediator. A United Nations Security Council resolution gave Jarring the mandate he needed to negotiate a peace, yet in many respects tied his hands by spelling out the bases on which it was to be negotiated: withdrawal of Israeli armed forces from the territories they acquired in the war; termination of all claims of all belligerent states on territories of others; recognition of secure boundaries and the rights of all countries to live free from threats or acts of force; guarantees of freedom of navigation of all waterways (including the Suez Canal); a "just settlement" of the refugee problem; and demilitarized zones to guarantee the territorial integrity of all states in the area.

Within hours after receiving his mediation mandate from Secretary General Thant in 1967, Ambassador Jarring was on his way to the Middle East. He spent more than a year shuttling between the various Arab and Israeli capitals and conferring with the major powers that held influence over the governments in the area. Finally, by dredging up the Rhodes Formula, he was able to convene the first peace conference on the Middle East in more than twenty years on August 25, 1970.

Sitting in his glass-walled offices in the United Nations Secretariat Building in New York City, Dr. Jarring received the ambassadors of Israel, the United Arab Republic, and Jordan. The talks lasted less than two weeks. On September 6 the Israeli cabinet, under the leadership of Premier Golda Meir, decided to withdraw from the talks until new missile installations, reportedly established with Soviet assistance in the Suez area, were removed.

The atmosphere during the talks had not been good. The Israelis continued to be suspicious of the truce in effect because they felt it gave the Arabs a chance to rebuild their defenses. And the Arabs feared the political consequences in their own countries of granting any concessions to Israel —even recognition of Israel's existence.

Again, it was a decision made by the heads of state that destroyed the talks. The Israeli cabinet's decision to "suspend" the discussions destroyed the years of work by Jarring to get the two sides to separate conference tables. It took another four months and his threat to withdraw as mediator before he could again convene the contorted discussions that passed for peace talks.

When the Rhodes-type talks resumed on January 5, 1971, Secretary General Thant issued a report on his mediator's efforts to that date. The report was grim—two belligerent camps still faced each other across the Suez Canal and along the other armed borders between Israel and the Arab world. But it was spiced with some optimism, since both sides had agreed to a cease-fire along the Suez. They had also agreed to seek a lasting peace on the basis of the 1967 Security Council resolution. This meant that Israel acknowledged, in principle at least, its withdrawal from conquered territories, while the Arabs acknowledged, in principle at least, recognition of the territorial integrity of Israel.

The talks begun again early in 1971 stalemated after a

few months over the issues of navigation of the Suez and Israeli occupation of Egyptian territory. By the end of March, Jarring had resumed his duties as Swedish ambassador to the Soviet Union, suspending, in effect, the deadlocked discussions. The following December, U Thant called for a reactivation of the Jarring mission, but the Egyptians and Israelis could not be brought together.

In the summer of 1972, after Egyptian Prime Minister Sadat had expelled Soviet military forces and advisers from his country, Golda Meir proposed direct talks with Egypt. Sadat rejected the offer, however, saying that the Big Four (United States, Soviet Union, France, and Britain) would have to participate in any discussions between Egypt and Israel. The Israelis opposed such participation, since they feared it would result in an "imposed settlement."

In the meantime, numerous incidents of terrorism, including the kidnapping of nine Israeli athletes at the Munich Olympics in September 1972, increased tensions in the Middle East. And despite reports of sporadic contacts between Israeli and Jordanian officials in London, prospects for a lasting peace in that part of the world seemed as remote in 1973 as they had been in 1967.

I have never been so convinced as now of the usefulness, the potential and the absolute necessity of the United Nations. The organization is evolving . . . through a process of trial and error toward a goal and an ideal which all can accept.

U Thant, 1971

Chapter Six **Brushfire Wars and World Peace**

On May 18, 1966, Secretary of Defense Robert S. McNamara told a meeting of the American Society of Newspaper Editors in Montreal, "In the last eight years alone there have been no less than 164 internationally significant outbreaks of violence—each of them specifically designed as a serious challenge to the authority, or the very existence, of the government in question."

Involved were eighty-two different governments, the secretary of defense said, and "not a single one of the 164 conflicts has been a formally declared war. Indeed," he added, "there has not been a formal declaration of war—anywhere in the world—since World War II."

Whatever they are called—local insurgency conflicts, brushfire wars, wars of national liberation—these violent outbursts are nevertheless major threats to world peace, or at any rate, major threats to the safety and well being of millions of innocent people.

Brushfire wars are very specialized types of conflicts. Generally they are conducted to liberate a country from a colonial master, thrash out a local border dispute, or settle extralegally the question of who will rule a given country. Because of the peculiar nature of each brushfire war, therefore, the nature of the brushfire peace that follows must be specialized as well.

Since World War II, there have been about fifty moderate- to large-sized brushfire wars. The statistics quoted by Secretary McNamara were a bit misleading. Eliminating one-shot incidents across the Berlin wall, for example, leaves several dozen incidents that could be termed wars and that called for some variety of peace afterwards. The Congo and Belgium, Cyprus and Great Britain, India and Pakistan are among the better known.

In *Last Reflections on a War* (1967) the late historian Bernard B. Fall, a leading expert on Vietnam and on insurgency wars, divided the kinds of peace that mark the end of brushfire conflicts into three categories—"the counterinsurgent wins; the insurgent wins; or there is a stand-off. In turn," he wrote, "each of the three categories can be neatly divided into 'talk' and 'no-talk' subcategories."

A look at the various brushfire wars since World War II shows that of the six possible combinations, the least common is the "no-talk" victory, unilateral battlefield victory by government forces. A ranking of the peace talks since World War II shows that the most common outcome is probably a negotiated or "talking" victory by the insurgent.

In Cyprus, the Congo, and along the India-Pakistan border there is some variety of peace today. A large part of the thanks for this is due to the United Nations, whose armed emergency peacekeeping troops enforced a truce while the diplomats and the politicians worked out a solution to the problems that had prevented a peace.

On Tuesday, August 16, 1960, at the first stroke of midnight, the Mediterranean island of Cyprus, under British control since 1878, received its independence. In the four years between 1956 and 1960, 508 people had died and 1,260 had been wounded in the violence that wracked the country. Archbishop Makarios, the Cypriot leader, had been imprisoned in a British jail, and three leading members of the Western defense community—Turkey, Greece, and Britain, all with rival claims to the strategic island—wrangled over its possession.

The conflict had begun nearly ten years before with sporadic guerrilla violence that ultimately brought thousands of British soldiers to the area. The two truces intervening before independence in 1960 were never really effective. The underlying emotional issue of Greek majority versus Turkish minority was not resolved, and time and again it flared into violence and resulted in death.

The amicable peace reached after eighteen months of negotiations and threats in London in 1959–1960 was short-lived. Though the governments in London, Athens, and Ankara managed to submerge their deep hostilities, guarantee Cyprus's territorial integrity, and keep their hands off the island, neither the Turkish minority population nor the Greek majority on Cyprus signed the treaty—indeed, they were never asked to agree to a peace. Within three and one-half years, by December 1963, the truce had collapsed, along with the peace treaty itself (known as the "Treaty of Guaranty") and the structure of government on the island.

Should the majority always rule?

This time the United Nations, flushed with a measure of success in the Congo, stepped in with force to make the peace. The United Nations peacekeeping effort in Cyprus was typical of the procedure employed by the organization in several of the major insurgency campaigns of the post-World War II era. First, the United Nations Security Council, faced with an outbreak of violence in a country, would convene a hasty post-midnight session at the New York headquarters. During the Cyprus crisis, Secretary General U Thant proposed a compromise plan of constitutional revision to protect minorities on the island, but in the intervening months of negotiation he urged the formation of a multinational armed force to keep both sides from each others' throat, by force if necessary.

The second step in the procedure was assembling a peace-keeping force—generally from nonaligned nations, often those with some interest in the area (African nations if the country in question was in Africa, for instance)—then appointing a mediator as a direct representative of the secretary general and through him the Security Council.

The final step was the bargaining itself, often lasting for years. The mediator would move back and forth between the rival camps trying to convince both sides to sit down with each other. Then, hopefully, the peace treaty was written and signed, and United Nations military forces remained only until order in the country was assured.

The first and second stages went without hitch in the Cyprus crisis. The United Nations force was established by Security Council resolution on March 4, 1964, and a short time later paratroopers arrived on the island, followed by mediator Sakari S. Tuomioja, former premier of Finland. He quickly established a base in Geneva and invited all parties to the dispute to discuss the question of peace. But he suffered a stroke and died that September before he was able to arrange a compromise.

Since then Cyprus has maintained its unquiet truce. United Nations forces continue, at a cost of millions of dollars per year, to keep whatever semblance of peace is possible on the island. Greek and Turkish guerrilla fighters in the mountains still prey on each other's population, but at the peace tables the stalemate goes on.

There has been no resolution of the question of who will rule Cyprus—the Turks or the Greeks. Each nationality has its own emotional tie, its own reason for wanting control of the island. The minority fears oppression by the majority, and the majority feels it is entitled to rule. Poised in a strategic area of the Mediterranean where Soviet and American warships constantly churn the sea, its continued placidity is crucial to prevent an East-West clash. Thus, neither the United States nor the Soviet Union has interfered, afraid to disturb the delicate balance. Again, the United Nations has manufactured an armistice, but not a peace.

Several thousand miles to the west and south, while United Nations forces were facing frustration and stalemate on Cyprus, the United Nations was scoring perhaps its biggest peacekeeping victory in the largest of the African nations, the Democratic Republic of the Congo.

The Congo became independent from Belgium on the last day of June 1960. King Baudouin flew in from Brussels, President Eisenhower sent a bust of Abraham Lincoln to the new government, and Dr. Ralph J. Bunche, now undersecretary for special political affairs, represented the UN at the ceremonies. It was a sunny day in Léopoldville and all was amicability. But Belgian officers commanded Congolese troops controlling all the ceremonial areas.

Within two weeks, disorders had flared across the country, triggered by tribal rivalries, desires by powerful Belgian economic interests to safeguard their investments, and the emergence of local leaders, such as Moise Tshombe of Katanga Province, who endeavored to pull their provinces out of the new nation.

But this time, there was a central government that considered itself in at least political, if not military, control of the situation. Within hours of Tshombe's secessionist proclamation in Katanga on July 11, 1960, Congo President Joseph Kasavubu asked the United Nations to assist in restoring peace. After a brief Security Council debate, Secretary General Dag Hammarskjöld organized a United Nations emergency force and, together with Dr. Bunche as mediator, airlifted troops into key areas of the Congo.

Within six months of the arrival of the United Nations force, the Congo was divided into at least four major factions, headquartered in the provinces of Katanga and South Kasai and the cities of Léopoldville and Stanleyville. Secretary General Hammarskjöld had established a United Nations Conciliation Commission in November 1960, and two months later, shortly after the first of the year, its members arrived in Léopoldville.

Throughout his tenure, it was the goal of Hammarskjöld to achieve a real peace, and, operating through a series of Security Council mandates, he instructed his lieutenants, particulariy Dr. Bunche, not to settle for a military occupation of the country. These peacemakers faced a string of powerful, often self-styled leaders, a bitterly divided neophyte country having no tradition of self-rule or self-help, and occupying Belgian troops and officials who served only to remind the Congolese in power that they were still only a half-step from colonial rule.

United Nations military forces quickly established order in the countryside. The mediators then moved to bring together the feuding elements. Within three months of their arrival in Léopoldville, United Nations mediation officials managed to get the two principal leaders, plus several other lesser figures, to the conference table—at Tananarive, Malagasy Republic—in an effort to form a confederation of Congo states. A month after that, at Coquilhatville, Tshombe broke up the conference, which had appeared on the road to a real agreement, by walking out in anger. The situation deteriorated when Central Government troops arrested Tshombe as he was about to board a plane back to his secessionist Katanga province.

It was not until Tshombe's military machine, small though it was, was crushed in January 1963 that a real peace was possible in the Congo. By this time, United Nations officials had managed to reinforce local rule by bolstering the authority of the Central Government, promoting a unity plan, and pouring development funds into the country.

By June 1964 the last of the UN troops had left, and the Congo was on the road to peace. It was a curious peace indeed. It was arranged more by the removal of mercurial leaders, whose temperaments had broken the tranquility of the country, than by any changes in ideologies or in the Central Government. And although the agreements on minor subtleties at the peace tables helped to soothe bruised egos, the peace was not in fact accomplished until some small battlefield victories by the United Nations force destroyed the remaining resistance.

Perhaps the major peace talks since World War II between the heads of state of two major countries took place in January 1966. The purpose of the talks was to settle what promised to be a major conflict on the borders of two of the most powerful nations of the world—the Soviet Union and Communist China. The disputants were India and Pakistan; since the 1940s they had been in disagreement over religious and colonial issues, and especially over the possession of a small slice of territory, Kashmir.

President Ayub Khan of Pakistan and Prime Minister Shastri of India met in the Soviet Asian provincial capital of Tashkent. It was an eyeball-to-eyeball confrontation, as a famous photograph of the time revealed—the silhouettes of the Indian and Pakistani chiefs of state outlined against the curtains of the negotiating room, staring straight at each other. Premier Kosygin of the Soviet Union, fearing war on the very doorstep of his nation, played the role of mediator, exulting when on January 10, 1966, a peace accord, the Tashkent Declaration, was signed.

The war had lasted, with heavy casualties, a little more than a month, in August and September of 1965, before United Nations Secretary General U Thant succeeded in calling a truce between the two countries. The Soviet Union took the initiative by bringing both sides to the peace table.

This was the first peace of the postwar period to be accomplished through direct pressure and intervention by a major power. The Tashkent Declaration, however, never resolved the key questions of the war—the status of the area called Kashmir and, above all, the ancient religious antagonisms of the two nations coexisting uneasily on the same subcontinent. So it has been a peace violated scores of times by minor border skirmishes between the two hostile states and finally by a major brutal, though short-lived, war between India and Pakistan late in 1971.

There were no peacemakers after the bloody war that established the new nation of Bangladesh in 1971, since peace was achieved by the muzzle of a gun. Each side had its major-power supporters—Pakistan had the People's Republic of China and the United States, and India had the Soviet Union. But no superpower was willing to commit itself totally to the support of either belligerent.

The peacemaking procedures following these three brush-fire wars—Cyprus, the Congo, and the 1965 India-Pakistan conflict—are typical of the methods used for settling such disturbances. On Cyprus and in the Congo, intervention by an impartial supranational body, the United Nations, accompanied by a judicious use of force, attempted to move both parties toward peace. In the former case it failed, but in the latter it worked satisfactorily after some hesitant starts. In the Congo, personalities played the key roles; on Cyprus, the clash of nationalities was crucial. In India and Pakistan in 1966, a combination of United Nations assistance and major-power intervention, coupled with a fortuitous interplay of personalities of the heads of state, brought a temporary peace.

Who are the world's peacemakers?

It would be extremely unwise for a responsible American official . . . to give a checklist about what the United States will or will not do in every circumstance that is likely to arise.

Henry A. Kissinger, 1973

The Vietnam peace talks in Paris should be sufficient evidence of the dangers of planning for the diplomatic future. When the delegates sat down across from each other at the Hotel Majestic in 1968, they had every hope and expectation that within a matter of months, if not weeks, there would be an end to the fighting and a lasting peace in Southeast Asia. In reality, the negotiations lasted five years while the fighting continued.

Nevertheless, from the United Nations in New York, to the most obscure university hall or "think tank," to the third floor of the Department of State Building in Washington, there are theoreticians still thinking about the future. Ten years ago, one such theoretician, a physicist with the prestigious RAND corporation, decided to forecast what peace or war might be like in the future. Herman Kahn began to play what are now called "strategy games," projecting in often complex mathematical formulae just what shape the future will take. In 1967, together with his colleague Anthony J. Wiener, he wrote *The Year Two Thousand*. In it the authors set up their war-peace scenarios for the first half of the next century.

They projected three alternatives to the "Standard World": 1) an *integrated*, relatively arms-controlled world; 2) an *inward-looking* peaceful world having little arms control or coordination among nations; 3) a world in greater *disarray*, troubled and violent. But before they went on to speculate on each of these possible alternatives, the authors

57

declared their "most important caveat . . . *almost any day has some chance of bringing up some new crisis or unexpected event that becomes a historical turning point, diverting current tendencies so that expectations for the distant future must shift.*"

The State Department's chief soothsayer, the head of the Policy Planning Council, agreed wholeheartedly with the Kahn-Wiener caveat. And it is for this reason, Assistant Secretary of State William Cargo said in a 1970 interview, that the planning functions of the United States in foreign policy simply do not look more than ten years in the future. "Very little practical planning can be done beyond five years," Cargo said. "If you stretch it to ten you're in real trouble. There's a mythology—projecting a long way ahead usefully. It simply can't be done."

The State Department's think tank, the Policy Planning Council, was set up by Secretary of State Marshall after World War II. Its first task was to draw up plans and projections for the Marshall Plan to aid postwar Europe, with the idea of keeping it non-Communist. Since then, the staff and its scope of operations have grown, until now it consists of nearly twenty full-time foreign service officers and their supporting personnel.

Lately its occupations have broadened until now it encompasses the entire area of American foreign policy. "We have here a group of people who look at United States foreign policy with the same overview that the Secretary [of State] must look at it," said Cargo. In 1970 the staff projected, for instance, the various diplomatic and military alternatives that could result in the Middle East from the various peace conference options. When Secretary of State William P. Rogers toured the area in May 1971, conferring with the various Midde East heads of state on the question of reopening the Suez Canal, he was thoroughly familiar with the projections of future possibilities.

Across Washington from the Department of State Building another agency serves a similar purpose for the president of the United States—the National Security Council, headed by National Security Adviser Henry A. Kissinger.

Kissinger is one of the few academics (another was his predecessor, ex-Harvard dean McGeorge Bundy) who has had an opportunity to put his ivy-covered musings into practice on the international scene. His theories developed and matured after the publication of his first major book, *Nuclear Weapons and Foreign Policy* (1957).

In that work, he stated that a limited nuclear war was not only possible but might even be a blessing to the United States, since survival for America "depends not only on our strength, but also on our ability to recognize aggression." That view changed; Kissinger now declares that nuclear war should be avoided at all costs. In his 1957 book he wrote on the subject of peace:

> Whenever peace—conceived as the avoidance of war—has been the primary objective of a power or a group of powers, international relations have been at the mercy of the state willing to forego peace. To entrust the fate of a country entirely to the continued good will of another sovereign state is an abdication of statesmanship; it means that survival is completely dependent on factors outside of one's control.

With a staff of seventy-three working in specially designed White House offices, Kissinger and the National Security Council attempt to determine how the world's stability might be maintained with United States assistance. A multiplicity of daily crises prevented him from accomplishing the long-range projections he had wanted to undertake when he initially accepted his post. However, he was able to give to President Nixon the broad context of United States foreign policy. The results were greater ability to plan for the future of peace in Vietnam, to project the likelihood of meaningful developments in the Middle East, and to plan beyond the daily cable messages to and from American embassies abroad.

Regardless of the value of all of these various projectional tools of the United States government—often matched in other countries by parallel institutions such as the American Studies Institute in Moscow—they are nevertheless provincial; that is, their purpose is to forecast the role of the nation in the future world, whether it is at peace or at war.

On First Avenue in New York there is one institution that seeks to forecast a *world of peace* for the future. Three successive secretaries general—Trygve Lie, Dag Hammarskjöld, and U Thant have made their goals the preservation of peace and, by judicious use of foreign assistance, diplomacy, and debate, the maintenance of an atmosphere of international consultation that will assure harmony in the future.

Is the UN the major peacemaking force in the world?

"The community workshop of the world" was the way its first chief executive visualized the United Nations. Two years after Trygve Lie presided at its christening in San Francisco in 1945, he told an interviewer, "We cannot fail. We have made a better beginning than most people realize. We must learn to think impartially, in terms of the world, to discard nationalisms. The world has such a long way to go! The statesmen have such a task!"

Lie's successor, Dag Hammarskjöld, also believed that the UN must succeed if world peace is to be preserved. Hammarskjöld realized as well that the best road to world peace was the judicious use of the power of the United Nations.

"It's a conviction that has to do with, well, church words, with a belief in a bond of morality and decency," he told A. M. Rosenthal of *The New York Times* in 1953, four months after taking over from Lie.

"There is a simple basic morality that motivates most people. The great moment is the moment of realization in people that their desire for decency exists not only in their own groups but in others. It is a difficult thing to get across, but it does get across," he said. "Someday, I know it, people will realize that the UN is a reflection of that desire and that if they tear it down, why, they will have to build it up again. And when that day comes they will say 'those guys there at the UN, they're all right.' "

Wherever Hammarskjöld sent United Nations troops during his years as secretary general, he thought of them always as peacekeeping troops. In the Congo, in the Middle East, in Cyprus, he made certain that while the troops might fight to keep order, they also sought to bring to these countries peace and the "desire for decency" that he felt the residents of the occupied nation wanted.

He died trying to bring peace to one of those nations—in the Congo in 1961. It was left to his successor, U Thant of Burma, to wind up some of the operations Hammarskjöld started—the Congo, for instance. U Thant too is proud of the contributions he has made to the world's peace—in the Indian-Pakistan border fighting, for instance.

"There are many things over which I am very gratified," he told an interviewer in 1969 on the eighth anniversary of what he called a lonely job, "a sense of satisfaction and a little accomplishment. I think I contributed in some way to the easing of the Cuban missile crisis. . . . I hope I am able to contribute a little bit to stimulate thinking, just to stimulate thinking to fashion a better world."

All of these people, from Kissinger in the White House to Kahn in his "think tank" to U Thant in his glass-walled offices in the Secretariat, are immersed in the day-to-day problems of peace and war in the world. They are also very much concerned with the world of the future—and the peace it may or may not hold. They are practical people, yet thinkers and theoreticians of the shape and fabric of peace. **Can peacemakers help** They hope that by determining the factors that influence **prevent wars?** the peacemaking process they can avert the next war or prevent the subversion of the next peace.

1. List four peace negotiations that were directly affected by the personalities of national leaders or diplomats. In which negotiations did personalities play a positive role? In which did they play a negative role?

2. Why was the Vietnam War not settled by a United Nations negotiating team? Under what circumstances is a settlement by UN negotiators *not* possible?

3. Since 1919 heads of state have taken over from diplomats the task of negotiating peace settlements. Why have they done so? Should full authority to make peace agreements be returned to professional diplomats? Why or why not?

4. Imagine a computer that could be programmed with all the information concerning a war and possible peace plans. Would you support a peace settlement drawn up by such a computer? What advantages and/or disadvantages would such a method have?

Bibliography

Bemis, Samuel F. *A Diplomatic History of the United States.*
5th ed. New York: Holt, Rinehart & Winston, 1965.

Fall, Bernard B. *Last Reflections on a War.* Garden City,
New York: Doubleday, 1967.

———. *Two Viet-Nams: A Political and Military Analysis.*
2nd rev. ed. New York: Praeger, 1967.

Kahn, Herman, and Wiener, Anthony J. *The Year Two
Thousand: A Framework for Speculation on the Next
Thirty-Two Years.* New York: Macmillan, 1967.

Kennan, George F. *Memoirs, 1925–1950.*
Boston: Little, Brown, 1967.

Kissinger, Henry A. *Nuclear Weapons and Foreign Policy.*
New York: Harper & Row, 1957.

Teltsch, Kathleen. *Crosscurrents at Turtle Bay: A Quarter-
Century of the United Nations.*
Chicago: Quadrangle, 1970.

Ulam, Adam B. *Expansion and Coexistence: The History of
Soviet Foreign Policy, 1917–67.*
New York: Praeger, 1968.

Editorial: Daniel H. Ryan
            Maridee Johnson

Design: James A. Buddenbaum
         Joan H. Menocal